Patricia Mello Saheli

The Formation of the Reflective Teacher

Patricia Mello Saheli

The Formation of the Reflective Teacher

Psychopedagogical Contributions

ScienciaScripts

Imprint

Any brand names and product names mentioned in this book are subject to trademark, brand or patent protection and are trademarks or registered trademarks of their respective holders. The use of brand names, product names, common names, trade names, product descriptions etc. even without a particular marking in this work is in no way to be construed to mean that such names may be regarded as unrestricted in respect of trademark and brand protection legislation and could thus be used by anyone.

Cover image: www.ingimage.com

This book is a translation from the original published under ISBN 978-3-330-75581-9.

Publisher:
Sciencia Scripts
is a trademark of
Dodo Books Indian Ocean Ltd. and OmniScriptum S.R.L publishing group

120 High Road, East Finchley, London, N2 9ED, United Kingdom
Str. Armeneasca 28/1, office 1, Chisinau MD-2012, Republic of Moldova, Europe
Printed at: see last page
ISBN: 978-620-5-07343-8

SUMMARY

DEDICATORY: 2

ACKNOWLEDGMENTS 3

SUMMARY 5

INTRODUCTION 6

1 METHODOLOGY 8

2 INITIAL PSYCHO-PEDAGOGICAL REFLECTIONS 10

3 (UN)BUILDING MYSELF 13

4 INSTITUTIONAL PSYCHOPEDAGOGY 15

5 THE REFLECTIVE TEACHER 18

6 REFLECTION AND EDUCATION 22

BIBLIOGRAPHICAL REFERENCES 42

DEDICATORY:

To my parents and my aunt Verônica:

Truly the greatest teachers I've ever had. They always believed in me.

To my husband:

For unconditional love.

My sister:

For their technical and sentimental support.

To my students:

For the chance to have had experiences with them that I will carry with me for the rest of my life.

To my teachers:

For becoming an educator.

ACKNOWLEDGMENTS

All a dream needs to come true is someone who believes it can.

Roberto Shinyashiki

I would like to thank all those who believed in my dreams and supported me in achieving the title I had so longed for in my career as an educator.

I thank God, who gave me strength and illuminated the most difficult moments of this journey.

To my parents, my first teachers, who showed me right from wrong, introduced me to the fascinating world of books and the wonder of learning.

To my husband, for his constructive criticism, support and encouragement to write about the subject that most draws my attention, teacher training.

My sister, who helped me so much with the technical side of this work.

To all my teachers, who directly or indirectly contributed to my choice of profession.

To my advisor, Dr. Neide de Aquino Noffs, for her patience and understanding and for teaching me how to be a woman.

To PUC-SP, where I found a welcoming environment and excellent infrastructure.

SAHELI, Patricia A. M. The formation of the reflective teacher: psychopedagogical contributions. Monograph (Specialization in Psychopedagogy). Pontifical Catholic University of Sao Paulo, Sao Paulo, 2012.

SUMMARY

This paper aims to research the formation of the reflective teacher from a psycho-pedagogical perspective, as well as to discuss one of the roles that can be played by the institutional psycho-pedagogue within the school. The aim is to reflect on the way we think and how this mechanism influences the educator's choices within the teaching-learning process. It presents some definitions of what it means to think, relating it to the teacher's teaching methods. The methodology used was qualitative, focusing on bibliographical research. The theoretical framework used was the conceptions of various authors on the subject, as well as personal reflections on the object being investigated. The results obtained highlight the importance of psycho-pedagogical intervention in the training of reflective teachers, as well as the need for more in-depth studies on the subject.

Keywords: Institutional Psychopedagogy; Psychopedagogue; Reflective Teacher; Learning; Teaching; Thinking.

INTRODUCTION

This work is the result of reflections based on the psychopedagogy study group supervised by Professor Neide de Aquino Noffs at PUC-SP.

The study group was an open space where it was possible to share common objectives and needs, through permanent dialogue about the institutional reality as it is, with a focus on learning, building collective and collectivized knowledge.

Institutional psycho-pedagogy offers an alternative way of integrating people, as well as a way of articulating school content, knowledge and teaching-learning activities.

We work with people who are constantly learning.

In order to carry out this work, we started from points inherent to the role of the institutional psychopedagogue, according to Noffs (2003, p. 132)

It manages anxieties, creates a harmonious atmosphere in working groups, collaborates with the construction of knowledge and identifies obstacles in the learning and development process, addressing the student as a learner and the teacher as a teacher.

Based on these assumptions, how can we carry out interventional work with teachers and future teachers, working on the link with knowledge?

Our aim is to present how the institutional psychopedagogue, based on reflective practice, can intervene in the teacher training process.

We understand that in the institutional environment, learning difficulties can also be generated or aggravated according to the conceptions adopted in the school by its educators.

Our object of study is the institution, as it is the physical space for learning, evaluating the didactic-methodological processes and the institutional dynamics that interfere with the learning process. The action of the psychopedagogue is centered on issues related to learning, not only of the student but also of the educators and others involved in this process.

One example is Ollerton (2006, p. 23)

A certain student recently asked me: "What makes someone a good teacher?"... "That's a weighty question. "How do I begin to answer it?" and "After all, what does it mean to be "good"? I gave an answer: "To be a good learner" (emphasis added).

To be a good learner is to know how to make sense of events, to perceive relationships between what we know and the new experiences we go through. Therefore, one of the characteristics of teacher improvement is "becoming better" at what you do.

Therefore, to paraphrase Noffs (2003), the psycho-pedagogue is the transformed pedagogue.

1 METHODOLOGY

For the research in question, we used the qualitative approach, which, according to Severino (2002), demands autonomous, creative and rigorous personal reflection from the researcher. The researcher gets involved in such a way that the object to be investigated becomes part of their life.

Minayo's (2007) idea of qualitative research complements what Severino (2002) says. For her, this type of research works with the universe of meanings, motives, aspirations, beliefs, values and attitudes. This set of human phenomena is understood as part of social reality, because people differ in the way they act, think and interpret their actions based on the reality they experience and share with their peers.

The qualitative approach delves into the world of meanings and needs to be interpreted by the researcher, who is influenced at the same time by the texts he reads and by the values and beliefs he holds as a result of his experiences.

Within the ideologies that guide the thoughts of the authors mentioned above, it is impossible to carry out research while remaining neutral. In bibliographical research there is a constant interlocution between the researcher and the text. This active work of reading and reflection enabled us to produce knowledge on a subject about which we had many questions. Many of these questions were clarified in this research. Others gave rise to new questions, which could certainly become new objects of research.

Therefore, my source of data was obtained through bibliographical research by consulting books, magazines, websites, articles, in short, various types of bibliography on the subject of learning difficulties.

It is worth pointing out that the research was theoretical in nature. The fact that it is considered theoretical is due, according to Minayo (2007), to the knowledge built up scientifically on the subject in question by other scholars before us and which currently serves as a source.

In this case, the studies carried out by Dewey, Schon, Morin and Noffs helped us to understand the chosen theme.

In short, this work has been built up through a spiral process that began with some questions, which were clarified as we developed this study.

2 INITIAL PSYCHO-PEDAGOGICAL REFLECTIONS

"Putting wings on caterpillars doesn't give rise to butterflies - it creates strange, inept caterpillars instead. Butterflies are created by metamorphosis". (MARSHALL, s/d apud DAViEs; EDWARDs, 1999).

In 2009, when I joined the psychopedagogy course offered by pUc-SP, I was able to begin a kind of investigation that was divided into two stages: the first through the observation I made while attending the course classes and the exchange of experiences with professional colleagues, and the second through my own participation as an English language teacher in primary and secondary schools.

My participation in classes was always specifically focused on teacher training. I no longer felt like just another English teacher, but rather a reflective teacher and researcher, concerned about the teaching-learning process and, above all, how I was transmitting knowledge to my students.

I have always sought to improve my teaching practice, because through classroom observations and participation in training courses, I realized that my main objective was to analyze the problems brought up by my fellow teachers, who, like me, seek autonomy, creativity and freedom in the teaching-learning process.

I became very concerned when I realized that the challenge faced by teachers who are committed to their pedagogical practice is not just to choose an ideal methodology for teaching and learning, using ready-made formulas that are reflected upon mechanically, but that the great advance has its origins in the training of research and reflective teachers and in the analysis of the problems brought up by teachers in training courses.

Faced with this reality, my research question arose, which I sought to investigate in order to better understand the relationship between psycho-pedagogical contributions to the training of reflective teachers and their future performance and participation in the classroom.

how can reflection help elementary school teachers in their pedagogical work?

Considering that Pedagogy is a science whose objective is reflection, we then take as our starting point: How can we train reflective teachers?

The aim of this paper is to present part of the bibliographical research, the psycho-pedagogical focus that aims to favor the construction of autonomy through reflective practice. In order to develop the theory, authors from the fields of psycho-pedagogy, reflective practice and pedagogy worked together.

The motivating idea for the topic was a reflection of my own concerns in collective coexistence, with the paths of education and reflection, as a teacher and as a psychopedagogue, what changes can I bring to contribute to the educational environment?

This question will permeate the entire process of this final year's work.

Answering this question brought me back to my own questions and "reflections" on the subject.

I used a wide variety of readings to reach a conclusion on what was raised and I can say that this is an answer in the making, without defined limits, in a constant process of maturing and thinking about what it is to be this teacher and questioning practical situations as the basis of their training.

In a unique way, research into professional teacher training has deconstructed certainties and, above all, has revealed different possibilities for study and research, because, to the extent that they question merely technical training, they indicate new training paradigms based on the understanding that the training process alone does not ensure the effective professional preparation of teachers, how to articulate this need with the opening up of the field of institutional psychopedagogy?

Today, psychopedagogy is gaining ground and importance in society, with the psychopedagogue being an ally not only in helping to improve learning, but also as a partner within institutions in helping to train teachers.

3 (UN)BUILDING MYSELF

Knowledge has often appeared to me as a cloud, something that is above us, high in the sky, that we admire but can't touch.

As an educator, I've always made a point of giving more, looking for different teaching practices, changing my discourse, reflecting on everything that was happening in my classroom and what I could do to change it. Sometimes putting our thoughts into words that are understandable to the students becomes a task that needs to be improved on a daily basis.

I found it a bit difficult to start writing, until I read a sentence that motivated me to start: "Learning to write is a matter of trusting what you have to say and not dreaming of the complete solution" (PIZA, 2011).

How can I build myself as a professional when I haven't yet built myself as a human being? How can I think about the difficulties I encounter along the way when I haven't yet managed to deal with my own difficulties?

How can I teach differently if I teach the way I learn?

I intend to give new meaning to teachers' experiences of teaching and learning, and this is one of the focuses of the research and work of Institutional Psychopedagogy that I propose in this work.

This subtitle is in the first person precisely because it includes me in the *hall of* the object of my study.

To think differently is to be open to new ideas and constructions. Many times when I've been invited to continuing education courses, methods and the like, I've found myself wondering how much this new knowledge will change my practice and application in the classroom.

I've always thought that there's a "filter" inside us that chooses what we like best or what we believe in. It's like a kind of eyeglass, which, when it's at the "right" degree, helps, but if someone uses an eyeglass whose degree is not their own, or tries to read with someone else's glasses, we can have uncomfortable results, a distorted view of reality. What will make us truly learn and teach? I confess that I have some difficulties in letting myself be convinced and applying new knowledge, new methodologies, in new situations.

How can I reinvent myself as an educator? I feel like an educator in the process of construction. Is my inner content letting the process flow naturally? I'm talking about understanding, as a learner, in the direction of meaning myself as a teacher.

4 INSTITUTIONAL PSYCHOPEDAGOGY

Psychopedagogy is looking for a clear identity, and among the issues involved in this process is the distinction of roles between clinical and institutional psychopedagogy, according to Noffs (2003, p. 112)

After these studies, it is possible to envision psychopedagogy as an area of knowledge that studies and deals with the process of teaching and learning. This process takes place in various places: schools, hospitals, clinics, etc. When this process takes place within the school institution, we see that it requires a clarification of its trajectory.

And he points out: "Institutional psychopedagogy at school is the study of the learning modalities triggered and/or made possible by the School Institution".

Institutional psychopedagogy must look at the institution as a whole, in this case the school, and think about what to do within it.

We realize that training with a clinical bias leaves psychopedagogues ill-informed about their role within the institution.

Let's remember that being an institutional psychopedagogue is not about copying the modus operandi of psychologists, social workers, speech therapists, etc. The subject of psychopedagogy is the subject of learning, not the psychological subject.

Teaching what it is to learn and how to learn are some of the strategies of psychopedagogy in the process of institutional intervention. It is through the psychopedagogue's observation and the reflections generated by the group under intervention that the process linked to the issue of learning modality - teaching - is concentrated.

Noffs (2003, p. 71) points out that:

Therefore, to talk about teaching is to explain the mediations made by teachers between the components of their plan (objectives, content, strategies and assessments) and their students. The way of dealing with mediations generates learning. We can say that learning depends on how these mediations are made by the teacher.

From this explanation we can think: what image is the teacher making of themselves as a learner?

We can now move on to the question of learning and teaching modalities.

According to Schon (2000, p.99) "For fear that students may misunderstand, misuse or misappropriate it, these instructors tend, sometimes unconsciously, under the guise of teaching, to withhold what they know".

If within a so-called "normal" learning modality the teacher shows and has the freedom to "show" or "keep", in the pathogenic learning modality, the teacher hides knowledge.

It is also possible to observe the issue of the teaching method, loaded with personal values, in Morin (2011, p. 20) "This knowledge, which is both translation and reconstruction, involves interpretation, which introduces the risk of error in the subjectivity of the knower, their view of the world and their principles of knowledge".

How to transform teachers with pathogenic teaching methods?

Leading them to reflect on and become self-aware of their learning and teaching methods.

Agreeing with Noffs (2003, p. 77)

Teaching means enabling others to learn. Such teaching requires people who, in order to construct their own thinking, their own learning, have lived experiences as tools for this construction, an open attitude towards the new, a willingness to change, significant knowledge built up and the humility to recognize and face up to mistakes. Errors encountered during the construction of knowledge.

Teachers need to work on their values, because education is lagging behind other sciences. Trying to make the school aware of the models adopted is becoming urgent.

The psychopedagogue works by providing the school with the means to look at itself and discover who it is.

Institutional psychopedagogy can deal with teacher training, with support rooms, research and discussion groups, managing anxieties, looking for the learner within the teacher.

We can see that what changes within school institutions is the profile, but the model of the institution remains the same.

The psychopedagogue has the possibility of creating a reflective space in which teachers can think about their teaching difficulties, starting from their own history - the construction of a transformative narrative, understood here as the construction of other narratives, which allow them to reorganize their pedagogical practice, generating new possibilities for understanding personal, relational and educational experiences.

We believe that one of the roles of the institutional psychopedagogue is to provide moments of introspection, using resources that provide each person with the necessary conditions to analyze their own degree of maturity and commitment to the educational and personal process.

We believe that there is an urgent need to awaken a critical, analytical and reflective awareness in future teachers so that, once they have graduated, they are able to disseminate this practice as professionals.

5 THE REFLECTIVE TEACHER

Who is a reflective teacher? How can we define them?

This is a teacher who doesn't work with previous definitions, ready-made solutions, in other words, with a teaching manual. The reflective teacher is the one who is always questioning their practice, always seeing their relationship with their students and with knowledge as a "problematic" relationship, something to be resolved, something to be solved, for which we don't have ready-made solutions, we have to create hypotheses and test them.

Reflection should be seen as a tool for professional improvement.

Reflection is one of the dominant trends in the field of teacher training, and the concept of reflective practice emerges as a possible way for teachers to reflect on their teaching practices.

As Alarcâo (2010 p. 44) points out, "The notion of a reflective teacher is based on an awareness of the capacity for thought and reflection that characterizes human beings as creative and not as mere reproducers of ideas and practices that are external to them".

Reflecting on their practice, their work, their educational thinking, their working conditions, their identity as a professional, taking on the role of what they do, reinventing and leading actions.

Reflection is based on experiences. Analyzing these experiences makes it possible to look for more appropriate forms of practice and didactic alternatives to deal with problem situations in order to promote learning. Reflection is the search for ways to generate confidence and promote knowledge that is theoretically solid through work, transforming practice and going beyond mere doing.

They all start from the idea of a "reflective school", as an analogy to a widely used concept: that of a "reflective teacher". In this way, a reflective school would be conceived as one that thinks about and evaluates itself in relation to its pedagogical project and its social mission, constituting a learning organization that qualifies not only those who learn in it, but also those who teach in it, as well as all those who support teachers and students.

In the bibliographical survey process, we tried to compile a list of authors who could provide answers to our concerns. We compiled a fairly extensive bibliography and tried to identify the authors whose theories satisfied us, selecting John Dewey, Donald Schon, Edgar Morin, Philippe Perrenoud and Isabel Alarcao.

Reading their works and wanting to understand the concept of the reflective teacher, we came across the thinking of John Dewey, followed by Donald Schon and his fundamental notions. When Schon talks about knowledge in action, reflection in action, reflection on action and reflection on reflection in action, he summarizes that reflexivity is a competence that will provide educators with the conditions required to analyse, understand and improve their knowledge, contributing to the integral formation of their students.

We structured our work on the basis of definitions that helped us build a path and, as we ventured along it, we realized that the forks led us through an intricate process that, starting from the simple definition of education and reflection, went through the development of the teacher as an educator, his pedagogical practice and his performance, ending up in the school, the environment of knowledge par excellence.

We realize, then, that teachers are not allowed to build anything on their own.

It depends on the school, with its complexity, antagonisms and contradictions, to grow.

And a teacher's growth begins much earlier. If the teacher, during their academic training, develops the habit of reflecting on their own training, not just that acquired in the classroom, but their daily training, learned from their research, reading, discussions and participation in events and seminars on education, they will be forming a body of knowledge that they will carry throughout their lives and that will be improved every day, constituting the differential required to be, in fact, an educator, a reflective teacher.

And this reflective teacher brings with him the satisfaction of forming and changing, and this not only in relation to his students, but also in relation to his own person, as a human being who possesses knowledge, as long as it is articulated and organized.

Morin (2011, p 16) states that:

The supremacy of fragmented knowledge according to disciplines often prevents the link between the parts and the whole and must be replaced by a mode of knowledge capable of grasping objects in their context, their complexity, their whole.

And he emphasizes:

It is necessary to develop the natural aptitude of the human spirit to place all this information in context and as a whole. Methods must be taught to establish the mutual relationships and reciprocal influences between the parts and the whole in a complex world.

This is referred to by Morin (2011, p.16) as "pertinent knowledge", which can be multiplied through a relationship of exchange with your peers and, above all, with your students, i.e. it is not enough to have access to information, but you must learn to organize and articulate it. Isolated knowledge is not functional.

For this reason, education needs to help people understand and conceive of the relationships between the parts of knowledge and the whole/parts relationship.

This exchange relationship is facilitated in the school environment. The diversity found there contributes to creating, as we have already seen, complexity, antagonisms and contradictions, factors that provoke conflict, generate change and determine evolution. It is also in this environment that information and knowledge coexist and where otherness can be developed. Students need to see this environment as an opportunity to grow and learn and it is precisely the reflective teacher who will awaken their curiosity about this fact, making it a pleasant and rewarding experience.

The teacher and the school need to convey to the students the true meaning of teamwork, because one can't survive without the other and both can't survive without the student. The teacher and the school need to be partners, because they are part of the same community in which the student is the main protagonist. The school needs to be reflective, to grow, to be a favorable environment and a place for building knowledge.

6 REFLECTION AND EDUCATION

The first goal of education is to create people who are capable of doing new things and not simply repeating what other generations have done - people who are creative, inventive and discoverers. The second objective of education is to form minds that can be critical, that can verify and not accept everything that is offered to them. The greatest danger today is of "slogans", collective opinions, "ready-made" thinking trends. We have to be able to resist, [...] to criticize, to distinguish between what is demonstrated and what is not. We therefore need active disciples, who learn early on to find things out for themselves, partly through their spontaneous activity and partly through the material we prepare for them (PIAGET, 1987).

In the epigraph, Jean Piaget makes us stop and reflect on the creative capacity and responsibility of the educator in preparing and selecting the material to be used for the student's learning. However, when we talk about material, it is almost never imagined that the preparation of the educator himself is a practice inherent to this concept, since he is responsible for training. And that means giving the individual the ability to distinguish between what is put in front of them and what really interests them.

It is not possible to reflect on what education is without reflecting on man himself (FREIRE, 1979).

When we talk about being reflective, we need to question the concept of the term, which leads us to an intricate process, because it is up to the teacher to reflect on the content of their teaching, on the context in which what they teach is based, on their competence, methods, aims and objectives of everything they teach and, on the other hand, it is up to the student to reflect on their learning, on the relevance of this to their life, to their education, to their growth, on how much it adds to their education. Not that this will turn the student into a rebel who rejects the master's teaching, but into an individual capable of thinking, discussing, criticizing and contributing to the transformation and improvement of education.

Reflection and education are terms that evoke a sense of transformation, because they are characteristics of individuals capable of thinking. To think is to exist, to be a person, to live in a real world, to have a relationship with that world and to interact with it. "This relationship between man and reality, man and the world, [...] implies the transformation of the world..." (FREIRE, 1979, p. 17).

The reflective teacher, as the subject of this process, needs to be integrated into this "man-reality, man-world" relationship, because it is up to him to work with the individuals who are part of this relationship, in which he also participates. If teachers are not constantly concerned with their own preparation, how can they fully exercise their role?

The ideas of John Dewey and Donal Schon have influenced the field of education and those interested in teacher training.

Thinking, particularly reflective thinking, is essential for the learning of both teachers and students.

In recent years, reflection has suffered a loss of meaning. The fact that it has become everything to everyone has meant that it has lost its ability to be seen for what it really is.

One of the problems is the exact definition of reflective thinking. We can list at least four problems associated with the lack of a clear definition of reflection. Firstly, it is not clear how systematic reflection is different from other types of thinking. Does mere participation in a study group or keeping a diary, for example, qualify as reflection? If a teacher wants to think reflectively about their practice, what do they do first? How do you know if you're evolving or improving by doing this? What should teachers aspire to?

This leads to a second, concomitant problem: assessing a skill that is vaguely defined. With the demand for portfolios, for example, that demonstrate reflective thinking and practice, what, exactly, are we looking for as evidence of reflection? Are deep personal thoughts enough or are there specific criteria that can guide an assessment?

Thirdly, without a clear picture of what reflection looks like, it becomes difficult to talk about it. The lack of a common language means that talking about reflection is either impossible, or practitioners use terms that are common but have different meanings, or are different but have overlapping meanings (e.g. reflection, questioning, critical thinking, metacognition).

Last but not least, without a clear sense of what we mean by reflection, it is difficult to research the effects of reflective teacher education and professional development on teacher practice and student learning, and this is an essential issue.

Dewey reminds us that reflection is a complex, rigorous, intellectual and emotional endeavor that takes time to do well.

In this paper we look at different criteria that characterize Dewey's view of reflective thinking and offer them as a starting point for talking about reflection so that it can be taught, learned, evaluated, discussed and researched, and involves both meaning and utility.

We don't seek to codify or consolidate it, or to have it added to the list of standards to be met and tested. Our purpose is simply to provide a clearer picture of Dewey's original ideas, so that it can serve us when we improvise, revise, and create new means of meaning derived from experience - thinking to learn.

In his book *How We Think (1979)* Dewey identified various modes of thought, including belief, and stream of consciousness, but the mode he was most interested in was reflection.

The encounter with Dewey's prose becomes laborious and in order to make his theory a little more accessible we have tried to present some basic criteria present in his work:

- Reflection is a meaning-making process that moves the learner from one experience to another with a deeper understanding of their relationship to and towards other experiences and ideas. It is this connection that makes the continuity of learning possible, and ensures the progress of the individual. It is a means to essentially moral ends.

- Reflection is a systematic, rigorous and disciplined way of thinking with its roots in scientific research.

- Reflection needs to happen in community, in interaction with others.

- Reflection requires attitudes that value the personal and intellectual growth of oneself and others.

As Dewey defines it, reflection is a particular way of thinking and cannot be equated with mere chance or the state of "mulling over" something. Such thinking, in contrast to reflection, can be defined as undisciplined thinking.

Although the author clearly values reflection as the way to learn, at the same time he doesn't abandon other types of thinking, recognizing that they often serve the very issues that reflection can tackle productively.

Stream of consciousness is the thought that we are all involuntarily flooded with all the time. An uncontrolled stream of ideas in our heads.

Dewey (1979, p.14):

Whenever we're awake, and sometimes when we're asleep, something is, as they say, going through our heads. During sleep, we call this kind of sequence a "dream". However, even in a state of wakefulness, we have dreams, daydreams, build castles in the air, let ourselves be carried away by even more idle and chaotic mental currents. "Thinking" is sometimes called this disordered course of ideas that pass through our heads automatically and unruly.

This is often the only kind of thinking teachers have time for.

Reflective thinking, in contrast, is made up of defined units that are linked together so that there is a sustained movement towards a common end.

Reflection is not simply a sequence, but a consequence - an order so consecutive that each idea engenders the next as its natural effect and, at the same time, builds on or refers to the predecessor. The successive parts of a reflective thought derive from each other and support each other, they don't come and go confusingly.

Dewey (1979, p. 18) emphasizes that

Reflective thought makes an active, prolonged and careful examination of every belief or hypothetical kind of knowledge, an examination carried out in the light of the arguments that support it and the conclusions it reaches... but in order to establish a belief on a sound basis of evidence and reasoning, a conscious and voluntary effort is required.

Dewey cites Christopher Columbus as a reflective thinker, noting that he must have concluded that the world was round rather than flat based on his experience as a navigator. The impulse to reflect is generated by an encounter with, and conscious perception of, the potential Meaning inherent in an experience.

For Dewey (1979, p.26), the act of reflective thinking should be an educational goal, its positive points:

Firstly, it is a capacity that emancipates us from action that is solely impulsive and routine. To put it more positively: thought makes us capable of directing our activities with foresight and of planning according to ends in view or purposes of which we are aware; of acting deliberately and intentionally in order to achieve future objects or to have control over what is, at the moment, distant and absent. By bringing to mind the consequences of different modalities and lines of action, thought lets us know how far we have come in acting. It converts purely appetitive, blind and impulsive action into intelligent action.

For Dewey (1979, p. 22) reflection covers two phases of the act of thinking, "(1) a state of doubt, hesitation, perplexity, mental difficulty, which gives rise to the act of thinking; and (2) an act of research, search, inquiry, to find material that resolves the doubt, settles and clarifies the perplexity".

Dewey makes a distinction between thinking and believing:

A belief refers to something beyond itself, by which its value is gauged: it makes an assertion about some fact, some principle or law. It means that a certain fact or law is accepted or rejected, that it is something proper to affirm or at least agree with. The importance of belief goes without saying. It encompasses all matters of which we have no certain knowledge, but in which we trust enough to base our action on them; and, equally, matters accepted as true, as knowledge, susceptible, however, to future enquiries - as has happened with much of what was, in the past, admitted as knowledge and now occupies the limbo of mere opinion or error.

When we have a deep belief in what we believe to be the absolute truth, because we have been taught that it should be so, aren't we doing the same by copying, because we believe it, the teaching model we have been shown? Later identified as the truth, and as a belief that if this is the way we learned, other people will learn too.

Dewey (1979, p. 39) differentiates between the fixed idea of belief and attitudes favorable to the use of better methods of investigation and verification, among them open-mindedness. On open-mindedness: "This attitude can be defined as independence from prejudice, partisanship, and other habits such as being closed-minded and unwilling to consider new problems and new ideas".

About belief:

Mental indolence contributes greatly to dampening the spirit against new ideas. The path of least resistance and least effort is a mental furrow that has already been traced. <u>Changing old beliefs is a painful task</u>. It is often a sign of weakness to admit that a belief we once held is wrong. We identify with an idea so much that it literally becomes a "favorite", in whose defense we advance, mentally blind and deaf to everything else. Unconscious fears also lead us to adopt purely defensive attitudes, which act as weapons, not only to block new conceptions, but also to prevent us from gaining access to new observations. The cumulative effect of these forces is to cloister the spirit and keep it away from new intellectual contacts that are necessary for learning.

The difference between belief and open-mindedness:

The way in which they can most effectively be combated is to cultivate that vigilant curiosity, that spontaneous search for what is new, which is the essence of an open mind. For if it is open only in the sense of passively allowing things to penetrate it, it will not be able to resist the factors of mental enclosure.

Below we illustrate the virtuous circle of teaching where the psycho-pedagogue, supported by Dewey's theory and his psycho-pedagogical tools, can help build the reflective professional in education.

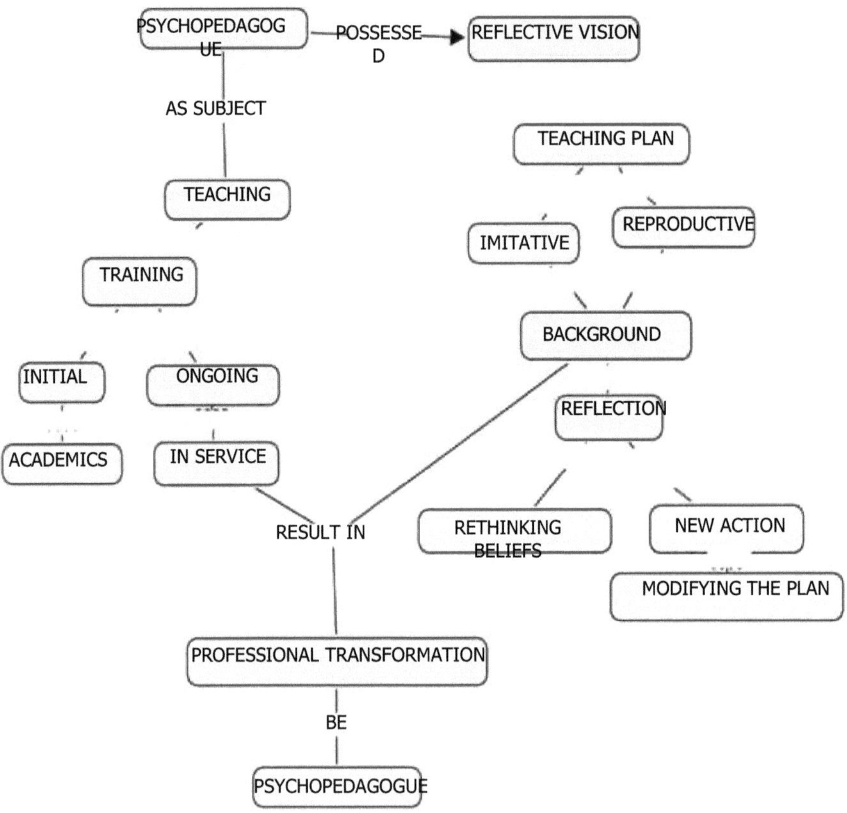

FIGURE 1: Construction of the reflective professional supported by the psychopedagogue. Map of ideas made using the cmap tools program (SAHELI, P.A.M. 2012).

Dewey (1979, p. 19) gives an example of reflective thinking using a brief explanation of a scene:

A man is walking on a hot day. The sky was clear the last time he looked at it, but now he notices that, while he is distracted by other things, the air has become colder. He thinks that it's probably going to rain; as he stares at the sky, he sees a dark cloud covering the sun and hurries on. Under these conditions, can we say that there has been a thought? Neither the act of walking nor the sensation of cold are thoughts. Walking is one way of directing activity; looking and noticing are other modes of activity. The probable rain was, however, something *suggested*. Our man feels the cold, *thinks of* the clouds, looks up, notices them and then thinks of something he doesn't see: a storm. This *suggested possibility* is the idea, the thought. If accepted as a legitimate possibility of occurrence, it becomes the kind of thought that falls within the scope of knowledge and requires reflective consideration (DEWEY, 1979).

We can conclude from the passage above that, if we consider thinking as a suggested possibility, we will be thinking about <u>predicting</u> the results of our attitudes and planning in relation to the teaching-learning process. It is at this point that the psychopedagogue, by implementing preventive resources, will enable the teacher to think reflectively and consequently rethink their role as the author of their knowledge.

For Dewey, thinking is a tool that we use in our practical, everyday lives. It's when we make use of ideas, data that we have, develop hypotheses to solve problems, test them and, depending on the result, confirm or not the main idea.

Reflective thinking is the same kind of thinking described above, but it is far removed from ordinary thinking. Dewey systematizes, in a more elaborate way, showing that there are a series of steps we can follow to verify our hypotheses, whether or not our ideas actually prove to be valid, in any case it is the practice and the result that will confirm or not our idea or thought.

Our impressions are in line with Noffs' (2003, p.129) thinking: "We must not forget that we are dealing with institutions and people who are in a constant process of learning".

The author defends the issue of autonomy, which is one of the objects of the psycho-pedagogue's research and work in the formation of authorship:

Ensuring autonomy of thought through a space in which the meanings of the group members can take place. A way of listening, looking and speaking that becomes psychopedagogical in the sense of allowing differences to present themselves (NOFFS, 2003, p. 129).

From an analysis of the above passage, we can see one of the focuses to be carried out by the institutional psychopedagogue in the direction of developing reflective thinking.

A strong belief that permeates the educational environment is that of the teacher as the "source of knowledge".

Fernàndez apud Noffs (2003, p. 38)

I make a distinction between knowledge and knowing. Knowledge is objectifiable, transmissible indirectly or impersonally, it can be acquired through books or machines, it is feasible, it must be systematized into theories, it is enunciated through concepts. On the other hand, knowledge is only transmissible directly, from person to person, experientially; it can't be learned from a book or from machines, it can't be systematized (there are no treatises on knowledge); it can only be enunciated through metaphors, paradigms, situations, clinical cases... <u>Knowledge gives power of use</u>. Knowledge doesn't. (emphasis added)

So if I'm the teacher, the source of <u>knowledge</u>, which has been passed on by someone else (another teacher), whom I admire, why should I change my belief that I can do things differently? We teach as we learn.

This seems to be a deep-rooted idea from which we can only be free through "discovering" and "recreating" ourselves as learners, thinking reflexively, opening the door to a dynamic knowledge capable of making our "beliefs" in educational methods and practices more flexible.

In the reflective process it is necessary to consider:

Reflection doesn't lie in the fact that one thing indicates another. It begins when we begin to investigate the suitability, the value of any particular index; when we try to verify its validity and find out what guarantee there is that the existing data really indicate the idea suggested in such a way as to *justify* accepting it (DEWEY, 1979, p. 21).

As Dewey (1979, p. 24) points out, "The need for the solution of a doubt is the basic and guiding factor in every mechanism of reflection".

Reflective thinking for Dewey (1979, p. 24) is not limited to the observation of facts or a "daydream" about a problem: "[...] the origin of thought is some perplexity, confusion or doubt. Thinking is not a case of spontaneous combustion: it does not come about in obedience to 'general rules'. It is something that causes it and provokes it."

Thinking reflexively in order to solve problems requires us to draw on our experiences and be in a state of perplexity, as Dewey (1979, p. 25) reiterates.

Given a difficulty, the immediate phase is to suggest some way out of it - to try to organize some plan or project, or to work out some theory that explains the particularities in question, to examine some solution to the problem. The data we have cannot provide the solution; it can only suggest it. So what are the sources of suggestion? Obviously, past experience and a wealth of useful knowledge. If we're familiar with similar situations, if we've dealt with a similar issue before, it's likely that we'll come up with more or less adequate and efficient suggestions. But if there is no analogous experience, confusion will remain confusion.

Even considering the factors of experience and bewilderment in relation to a given problem, it is still possible to fail to achieve reflective thinking due to the following factors:

It is possible, however, that we still don't think reflexively, even when there is a state of perplexity and a previous experience from which suggestions emerge. For it can happen that we don't exercise sufficient criticism of the ideas that occur to us; that we rush to a conclusion, without thinking about the arguments on which it is based; that we give up the search, the investigation, or shorten it unduly; that we adopt the first "answer" or solution that comes to mind, out of mental laziness, laxity or impatience to get to the end. We are only able to think reflexively when we are willing to endure suspension and overcome the drudgery of research. Many people dislike both the suspension of judgment and intellectual research: they want to see everything finished as soon as possible. They cultivate a mental habit that is excessively positive and dogmatic, or perhaps they fear that the condition of doubt will bear the stamp of mental inferiority. It is at this point, when examination and verification enter into research, that the difference between reflective thinking and misguided thinking becomes apparent (DEWEY, 1979, p. 25).

Following the line of reasoning about how we teach and how we learn, we come across the question of imitation.

For Dewey (1979, p. 65) in relation to the influence of other people's habits:

Just referring to the spirit of imitation in human nature will suffice to show how profoundly the mental habits of others affect the attitude of the student. Example has more power than precept, and so the teacher's best conscious efforts can be thwarted by the influence of personality traits of which he is unaware or to which he pays no attention.

We believe that there is a relationship of imitation from the teacher to the student, who, becoming the teacher, imitates the whole process, thus validating the other person's knowledge and comparing themselves to the holder of the same knowledge.

Following Dewey's observations on imitation, Schon (2000, p. 214) states that:

In fact, "Follow me" often tends to evoke negative reactions in both the instructor and the student whenever it becomes explicit. Even so, imitation is essential to learning and can be a creative act of considerable complexity. Paradoxically, it is blind imitation, rather than imitation as such, that most threatens students' autonomy; and it is blind imitation that students and instructors encourage when they maintain tacit imitation. To stimulate reflective imitation, instructors may need to invite students to reflect on their negative reactions to imitation.

The big question is, when in teacher training are we made to think critically about what is presented to us? What of what we have observed as practice is true and within our needs? How many of us

we don't wait for a manual with solutions just to be followed and not discussed or reworked.

Schon (2000, p. 214) raises the following question: "If skillful practice happens from meanings and feelings that are not under my direct control, how can I learn to create them?"

This is the great dilemma presented by the author on the question of imitation as such and blind imitation.

In the 1984 seminar, some students struggled explicitly with their dilemma. They tried to recognize and articulate the feelings and meanings that prevented them from achieving authentic practice, they reflected on the unfamiliar feelings they sometimes experienced when experimenting with new behaviors and, perhaps most importantly, they acted as if they were trying to learn not just a technique, but a new appreciative system and a new way of living, which each individual would develop in their own way (SCHON, 2000, p.214).

The role of the psycho-pedagogue in the question of imitation will be to discover the learner, the author, and how much of the imitation process is present in the educational practices of the teachers, and critically and analytically lead the teacher to discover their positive points within the process. The transformed teacher will have a psycho-pedagogical focus in their work.

According to Donald Schon (2000), professional practice is characterized by situations of instability and uncertainty that are not always resolved by the professional, as their repertoire of knowledge does not provide the answers required in the day-to-day exercise of the profession. These situations require the mobilization of knowledge and skills that go beyond the technical knowledge acquired in training processes.

In the Schonian perspective, reflection is based on lived experiences. Analyzing these experiences makes it possible to look for more appropriate forms of practice and didactic alternatives to deal with problem situations in order to promote learning.

Schon (2000, p. 32) states that when we learn something, we carry out the task without thinking too much about it. All experiences, whether pleasant or not, contain an element of surprise: when something doesn't meet our expectations, we can respond to it by reflecting on it in two ways: reflecting on the action, retrospectively examining what happened and trying to figure out how our action may have contributed to the result, or reflecting in the middle of the action, without interrupting it, calling this process reflection-in-action. At this point, our thinking can give a new shape to what we are doing while we are still doing it, so we are reflecting-in-action.

The author divides the criteria for reflective research into three: reflection in action, reflection on action and reflection on reflection in action, the first two of which are separated only by the moment in which they take place: the first occurs during practice and the second after the practice has taken place, in other words, when the action is reviewed and analyzed out of context. We become aware of the tacit knowledge in the reflection on the action and we reformulate our thinking in the action trying to analyze it, realizing that it is a natural act. Reflection on reflection in action is what helps professionals develop and build their personal way of knowing. It involves looking back at the action, reflecting on the moment of reflection on the action, in other words, what happened, what was observed, what meaning was attributed to it and what other meanings we can attribute to what happened (SCHON, 2000).

The author states that, based on the observation of professional practices, the reflective conversation that takes place during the action together with other participants or colleagues is the center of reflection on practice, and that these reflective conversations can collaborate and contribute to decision-making, understanding and the exchange of knowledge and experiences.

Reflection is associated with how we deal with the problems of practice, with the possibility of uncertainty, being open to new hypotheses, shaping these problems and discovering new paths, then arriving at solutions.

In his proposal for reflective teaching, Schon (2000, p. 23) points to the fact that professionals: "will have to learn to reflect on their own tacit theories, subject teachers on research methods; instructors on the theories and processes they bring to their own reflection-in-action".

It points out that professionals, instructors and researchers will have to study their own practice, and thus ask questions such as: what kind of people are willing, individually and collectively, to take on this practical and reflective stance?

"The development of reflective practical teaching can be combined with new forms of research into practice and education for that practice, to create a momentum of its own, or even something that is passed on by contagion" (SCHON, 2000. p. 250).

We understand that reflection provides teachers with correct and authentic information about their actions, the reasons for their actions and the consequences of their actions. Therefore, the quality and nature of reflection are more important than its occurrence. Teachers who reflect on their action are involved in an investigative process about themselves, as well as seeking to improve their teaching. This perspective assumes that teaching is a constant search with the aim of creating the conditions for learning to take place.

Reflective teachers have the opportunity to develop their practice on the basis of their own action-research within a school or classroom context, and this practice is underpinned by theories of education with which the teacher maintains a critical perspective. Reflection is an important element in the learning process, it is an integral part of the teacher's work and, in order to be understood, it needs to be part of the conditions and production of that work.

A teacher who doesn't reflect on his or her practice acts in a routine way, accepting the conditions and impositions. The reflective teacher seeks a balance between action and thought, and a new practice always implies reflection on experience, beliefs and values. Reflective action gives teachers an emancipatory power that cannot be dissociated from the social context in which they are inserted. This practice provides teachers with opportunities for professional and personal development.

Schon begins his speech by talking about the need for school reform, posing fundamental questions to be answered, for example: what are the skills that teachers should help students acquire? What kind of skills and knowledge should teachers have in order to do their job well?

He emphasizes the importance of professionals developing other qualities/intelligences, which he calls "artistic talent", such as insight, intuition, creativity and spontaneity. The "accumulation of knowledge" is not enough. It's no good just mastering content, theories, knowledge, without knowing how to apply it, use it, make it useful, solve problems and conflicts.

The expression *reflection-in-action* indicates that theory is inextricably linked to practice. It is the ability to respond to situations spontaneously, through improvisation. There are no ready-made technical solutions. The solutions to problems arise through the identification and conception of the problem, through the use of *artistic talent*.

And how do you develop "artistic" skills? The first requirement is freedom to learn through doing. This is what "reflective practice teaching" is all about.

The teacher gets in touch with what the students are saying and doing. They experiment.

The truth is that for a rich and profound proposal like that of the Reflective Professional, which he himself mentions is based on traditions, it couldn't be objective. Hence the importance of an epistemological approach to practice.

Schon points out that "we must stimulate and reward the development of the ability to teach". Considering the author's postulate, we can see the important role that the psychopedagogue can play in helping educators to discover themselves as learners and re-signify their role as teachers. The psycho-pedagogical professional can create ways of working collectively within schools, encouraging a reflective attitude. Psychopedagogy is based on a multidisciplinary vision, with the aim of demonstrating that, in the process of building knowledge, each subject uses their own ways of thinking and acting, unique ways of demonstrating the cognitive abilities present in their essence. The process of psycho-pedagogical intervention aims to offer the construction of autonomy through reflective practice.

Reflective practice opens up the possibility of engaging in professional improvement from the inside out. Reflection on practice is something we can do systematically and autonomously. Opportunities to work with someone else can lay the foundations for mutual support and collaborative action.

The implications for educators: the recognition of the effectiveness of their performance will depend less and less on the degrees obtained or years of repetitive practice.

7 THE INSTITUTIONAL PSYCHOPEDAGOGUE IN THE FORMATION OF THE REFLEXIVE TEACHER

In recent years, with access to school guaranteed for the majority of Brazilian children, there has been growing concern about improving the quality of education. There is a demand to improve the standard of classes, the use of new technologies and the inclusion of these students in the technological and information society. Our question is: As educators, are we prepared?

In order to meet this challenge, it is a priority and urgent that the school promotes changes in its structure, organization and, above all, in the pedagogical practices it develops.

Alarcao (2010, p.83) points out that:

Frustrated by the ineffectiveness of the concept of technocratic teachers, educators have become fascinated with the idea of the teacher as a reflective practitioner. But if teachers' lives have their own context, the school, it must be organized in such a way as to create conditions for individual and collective reflexivity.

Teacher training, whether initial or continuing, is therefore an important topic for study and research, in order to promote the conditions for schools to effectively fulfil their function of teaching and training citizens who are active in building a society that can, in Morin's words: face uncertainty, understand and be characterized by equity, justice and ethics.

In this context, Psychopedagogy, as an area that studies and deals with learning processes, cannot fail to be concerned with the issue of continuing education, not least because, among the various possibilities for the psychopedagogue to work, there is the supervision, elaboration or coordination of professional development projects for educators. the Psychopedagogue can be part of the school management team, concerned with the issues of reflection, learning and teaching.

Our experience shows that teachers, when evaluating training processes, often mention feelings such as being used as research objects, not being respected in their interests, needs, pace and process, or complain about the dichotomy between theory and practice on the part of the trainers and the lack of isomorphism between the training they receive and the type of education they are asked to develop. The trainers, for their part, point to teachers' resistance, fear of change, lack of commitment and failure in their initial training.

In our opinion, these explanations contain contradictions that leave doubts, as well as being simplistic and even reductionist, because they don't focus on the phenomenon in its many aspects.

Psychopedagogy is responsible for: reframing one's own learning in order to be able to teach, creating ways of working collectively within schools, in training courses and higher education courses focused on education, favoring a reflective practice.

An internship is offered at the university as part of our training as institutional psychopedagogues.

The institutional psycho-pedagogical internship was carried out on the premises of PUC-SP, with five second-year students on the Pedagogy course at the same institution.

The sessions were held in pairs, with one of the psychopedagogues preparing the meetings and the other observing the practice.

Under the acronym Napap (Nùcleo de Apoio Psicopedagógico à aprendizagem), the group was coordinated by Professor Dr. Neide de Aquino Noffs, director of the Faculty of Education and coordinator of the Psychopedagogy course at the aforementioned institution.

The psychopedagogical process lasted three months, with 11 meetings organized within the possibilities of PUC-SP's institutional schedule.

In the process of intervening with the future educators, we used autobiographical reflection, group dynamics, studies of academic texts, chronicles and magazine articles. We started from tacit knowledge to empirical and theoretical knowledge, which is necessary in academic training.

We use material pertinent to the pedagogy course in our consultations, combining it with the knowledge we acquired during our psychopedagogy training.

The psycho-pedagogical consultation with future educators opened up a big question for us about learning and teaching issues.

The first question we asked was why they had chosen to become educators. Two participants answered that they chose the course because they had an affinity with children, two others because it was accessible and easier, and one participant because of her political ideals.

Faced with the difference in interests regarding the course they were taking, the big question arose from the participants themselves: Am I prepared to teach?

From all the consultations, it was possible to see how concerned they were about knowledge and the lack of it for their academic achievements.

It took a while for the participants to stop calling us "teachers", they saw us as someone who possessed the knowledge and not as someone who was there to help them in the process of formation and re-signification as learners and later teachers.

There is a lot to be done in the field of institutional psychopedagogy.

One of the essential characteristics for this is the ability to think reflexively. In order to be reflective, you need to know and recognize yourself as a teacher, ask yourself about your practice and check whether it is in line with what you hold to be true.

Reflective practice is therefore: a process of making implicit actions explicit; a way of understanding classroom experiences; an approach to analyzing and rationalizing why we teach the way we do.

Becoming aware of your own practice or being explicit about implicit values is an important part of professional development. Recognizing and being aware of our values and basing them on existing practice leads to strengthening our teaching principles and makes us more secure about why we teach the way we do. Going through a process like this is getting to know ourselves. It means becoming more confident and more sure of our strengths and areas for improvement. The point is that, through reflective practice, through making notes on a few points, we can strengthen our pedagogy. In today's educational atmosphere of prescriptions and ready-made lesson plans, improving, deepening and strengthening pedagogy through reflective thinking is an essential part of professional autonomy, the key to personal satisfaction and a way of creating positive classroom environments.

Through our readings, we believe that psychopedagogy must establish an intimate dialogue with the disciplines of the educational field, since psychopedagogy is a transdisciplinary field. It is in the search for this dialogue with the different related areas and believing in a psychopedagogy that goes beyond a clinical approach, centered on learning difficulties and problems, that in this work we discuss the challenges posed in the current educational context for the training of educators in the reflective dimension.

The group discussions and the consultations led us to think about the true role of psychopedagogy within the school institution and that the reflective dimension is the way to work with adults, educators and trainers.

In short, for there to be reflection, there must be a problem, a question to be debated and resolved. The question is an unanswered fact and in answering it we use reflective thinking.

For Dewey, reflection must include action.

Reflection is not an end in itself, but a tool used to transform raw experience into meaningful theory that is based on experience, informed by existing theory, and serves the greater purpose of the moral growth of the individual and society.

It is an interactive process, going forward in a spiral movement, from practice to theory and from theory to practice. The process of reflection is rigorous and systematic, distinct from other thinking. It has its origins in the scientific method and, as such, includes precise steps: observation and detailed description of an experience, analysis of the experience, which includes generating explanations and developing theories, and experimentation - a test of the theory.

While reflection requires cognitive discipline, it also appeals to the individual's emotional dimension.

I reiterate the premise that Dewey was precise in his description of what it means to think reflexively. By adhering to the essential rigor inherent in his definition, teachers and trainers achieve different ends. Firstly, the process of reflection and the stages of observation and description, in particular, require teachers to confront the complexity of students and their learning, of themselves and their teaching, the subjects of their areas of knowledge and the contexts in which all of these operate.

Any action that the teacher takes, therefore, will be considered, rather than impulsive, a demonstration of in-depth knowledge of each of these elements and their interactions, which ultimately can only benefit the student's learning. Once teachers learn to think, they can teach their students to do the same, so that teachers teach best what they understand reflexively from their own experience. From this perspective, they can encourage their students to understand the phenomena of their world.

Reflection is a particular, defined form of thinking, which must be practiced.

Reflective thinking should not be understood as a sequence of disordered, unruly and automatic ideas, but rather as a conscious and voluntary effort based on an ordered set of ideas, an analysis of situations in the light of the arguments they support and the conclusions they reach. (deweyp. 18), because this is perhaps the most essential part of what makes us human, of what makes us learners.

In short, Dewey encourages us to think carefully about his theory of reflection, which should subsidize the individual and collective changes that our experience and knowledge reinforces in the educational paradigm: learning to think.

BIBLIOGRAPHICAL REFERENCES

ALARCÂO, I . **Professores reflexivos em uma escola reflexiva.** 2 ed. Sao Paulo: Cortez, 2003, 102 p.

DAVIES, M; EDWARDS, G. Will the curriculum caterpillar ever learn to fly? **Cambridge Journal of Education, v.** 29, n.1, p. 29, 1999.

DEWEY, J. **How we think.** How reflective thinking relates to the educational process, a re-exposition. John Dewey. New translation and notes: CAMPOS, C. H. 4 ed. Sao Paulo: Ed. Nacional, 1979.

FREIRE, P. **Educaçâo e Mudança**. 12 ed. Rio de Janeiro: Paz e Terra, 1979.

FREIRE, P. **Pedagogia da autonomia: saberes necessârios à pràtica educativa.**

Sao Paulo: Paz e Terra, 1997.

MINAYO, M. C. S. (org.) **Pesquisa Social. Teoria, método e criatividade.** 25 ed. Petrópolis: Vozes, 2007.

MORIN, E. **The seven knowledges necessary for the education of the future**. 3 ed. Brasilia: Cortez, 2011.

NOFFS, N. de A. **Psicopedagogo na rede de ensino: a trajectória institucional de atores-autores.** Sao Paulo: Elevaçao, 2003.

PERRENOUD, P. **Reflective practice in the teaching profession: professionalization and pedagogical reason.** Translated by SCHILLING C. Porto Alegre: Artmed, 2002.

PIAGET, J. **A linguagem e o pensamento da criança**. Sao Paulo: Martins Fontes, 1987.

PIZA, D. Do jà visto - Part I. **Folha de Sâo Paulo,** Sao Paulo, Feb. 21, 2011.

SCHON, D. A. **Educating the Reflective Professional: a new design for teaching and learning.** Translation: COSTA, R. C. Porto Alegre: Artmed, 2000.

SEVERINO, A. J. **Metodologia do trabalho cientifico.** 20 ed. rev. and ampi. Sao Paulo, Cortez, 1996.

43

SEVERINO, A. J. **Metodologia do trabalho cientifico.** 20 ed. rev. and ampi. Sao Paulo, Cortez, 1996.

I want morebooks!

Buy your books fast and straightforward online - at one of world's fastest growing online book stores! Environmentally sound due to Print-on-Demand technologies.

Buy your books online at
www.morebooks.shop

Kaufen Sie Ihre Bücher schnell und unkompliziert online – auf einer der am schnellsten wachsenden Buchhandelsplattformen weltweit! Dank Print-On-Demand umwelt- und ressourcenschonend produziert.

Bücher schneller online kaufen
www.morebooks.shop

info@omniscriptum.com
www.omniscriptum.com

Printed by Books on Demand GmbH, Norderstedt / Germany